Translating Mountains

In memory of Chris Reddick

Translating Mountains

Yvonne Reddick

Winner of the
Mslexia Poetry Pamphlet
Competition

Seren is the book imprint of
Poetry Wales Press Ltd.
57 Nolton Street, Bridgend, Wales, CF31 3AE

www.serenbooks.com
facebook.com/SerenBooks
twitter@SerenBooks

ISBN: 978-1-78172-420-0

A CIP record for this title is available from the British Library.

The publisher acknowledges the financial assistance of the Welsh Books Council.

Cover image: © Tbures | Dreamstime.com

Printed in Bembo by Berforts Ltd, Hastings.

Contents

At the Corrie of the Birds,

two figures emerge from lightless spruces,
one wraps a delicate arm around the other.

They scan a map of densely-contoured crags
for a chance that is becoming remote.

Stob Choire Claurigh – Peak of the Brawling Corrie

Just visible, the walkers scour
the feet of Caisteal's rock-fortress,
comb the heather that fledges
the base of its escarpment.
A pair of crows, circling.

Beinn na Socaich – Hill between Burns

Not a bootprint, no marks of a pole.
A rock at the falls' lip rolls, teeters –
cracks on gravel
with the noise a limb makes, on impact
with granite.

Teanga na Sine – Stormy Landspit

Two in the morning, and I jolt awake,
heart a trapped finch at my ribcage.

My mother pads across the floor above.
I rush upstairs to clasp her hand,
find it weightless as the quills of a wing.

Allt Choimhlidh – Stream of the Defile

Wet dawn surfaces at the window
like a drowned face still fixed in a smile.

The duty sergeant creaks up our staircase,
to tell us –
                    an animal cry
breaks from my lungs.

Coire nan Eun – Corrie of the Birds

The asphodels in late bloom,
at the dam, a bloated lamb
floats with its escort of flies.

One figure yells from the ravine's brink
as a mother hawk calls for a nestling
that opened its wings
and fell.

Sexton Beetle, Glen Feshie

Tangerine: vibrant
as a Calabari mask –
the shock of colour smudged
across your funereal shell, sexton beetle.

I wonder why you don't scuttle from me,
then notice that two mites are creeping
over your dried-out body.

An animal corpse will nurse your young.
You bury a fieldmouse,
embalm it, swaddle the crypt with its fur,
then feed its flesh to your larvae.
Your care for them has exhausted you.

The Peak of the Winds acts birdless –
not even a snow bunting breaks the stillness
as we slog up the slope over the winding Feshie.

This hill's crown is the last summit
where Dad and I will touch clouds,
he's unmistakable in black Gore-Tex
and red rucksack –
we return with our bones whole
from the path by the cliff-wall over Loch Einich,

and discover your vermilion and black husk
in damp grass, under the birches.

In five days' time, a helicopter
will spot Dad's rucksack.
The rescue team will dredge him from the stream –
at Raigmore Hospital, gloved hands will scurry
to set his mouth and eyes closed.

In ten days, he'll fly to England
where a dark-suited woman
in scarlet necktie and bug-eye glasses
settles him in his coffin.

She hands me a brochure of urns.

Sorrows of the Deer

I trace his last journey,
stepping deerlike
from Coire Choille
up the mottled hide

of the Peak of the Brawling Corrie,
down the heathery flanks
of the Point of the Fawn's Coombe
to peer into the stony cleuch
where the stream churns.

The day after he died
a wild hind watched me
from the birches by the Spey,
pricked her dished ears.

I need to weather brunt winds,
stolid as a tor
where mizzle pools and trickles –
I am hornless,
the wind stings through my fur.

That granite notch
in the Peak of the Pelts
is Ossian's – Fawn's – Cave.
I crouch under its dripping walls.

I want to endure,
a cup-and-ring marked stone,
the ancient landmap
of a spring's upwelling.

But a week after his death
I drive with my sister through Warfield
where a young roe
stares fly-eyed from the verge.

The gully is lush
with bracken and spotted orchids –
a smirr of rain
stains the afternoon
as we commit him to fire, to air.

Risk

The way he carried two compasses
in case one failed,
spare batteries for the GPS,

and jotted each leg of the journey
on an envelope, in a left-handed scrawl
no-one else could decipher.

The way he turned back
from the plateau of Wyvis
as clouds were glooming

and my friend's pack was a dead weight
of hairbrushes and spare socks;
tackled the Buachaille and the Ben

by the least craggy routes,
shunned cliffs, snow cornices.
(I was the one who tobogganed

down June snowfields, whooping.)
He rushed to save his camera first
when he fell chest-deep

into a stinking peat-bog,
and hoarded all his Ordnance Surveys
going back to 1976.

The way what came back
was a map, still legible
despite the bleeding ink.

A sealed survival bag.
His damp wool hat and gloves.

On the Alaskan Peak We've Never Climbed,

he dodges a cottage-sized boulder
of splintering granite:
"Tuck your head in!" to me below,
"Hang on!" my left fingers scrabbling at holds,

right hand clawing to place a cam
as the groaning rockfall
dims the sun overhead.
Earth shudders to a standstill

and I haul myself to join him
on the cropped grass of the col,
hand quaking in his.
There, to the west, is his mountain –

its horseneck ridge crested with pines,
head in a cowl of storm.
His hair has grown
from grizzled to deep brown

and death has washed him of fear
in the mapless land we track in my sleep.
A path winds westward
through barbed spruces –

he walks ahead, carrying the compass
that hangs on my wall,
turns back to beckon me, questioningly,
along the path I can't follow.

Howlet

Two nights before the inquest
we leave our dark-paned house
and hear her yelling in the forked chestnut
where Dad nailed the owl box.

Each foot a clench of grapnels,
she can hear our hearts
under yard-deep snow.
The barbs of her quills are hushed for flight.

Clutching the roof-tree
she turns her searchlight glare on us:
a *howlet*, an august eagle-owl
pricking her feathery horns when we stir.

We heard no voice but the wind's
through the phone, that last day –
when we rang, and rang, it was too late.
Now, she hovers over us, circling.

Look, I'm training her
to come to hand. I lure her
with a scapegoat house-mouse,
a chick's foot; feed her

until her street-lamp eyes
darken to beady brown
and she shrinks to the size
of a gentle tawny: *Jenny Houlet*
as the Scots call her.

Now, the tree stands empty.
She builds a twiggy mess
on the chimneypot over the cold hearth,
sits on brood.

Madness Lake

Not even when we gripped the clammy chain
to haul ourselves up the ice-scoured Dalle
did I think it was possible that you,

like a glacier, could change state
from solid to intangible
in the pause between my heartbeats.

Grinning and mopping your sunburnt brow,
you, my father, seemed imperishable
as the snow-hooded Pointe overhead.

When we reached the lake
the glacier calved with a gunshot,
jostled its floating bergs –

even then, its snout was retreating.
Twenty years to the day
since we last trekked this crisscross path

to Lac de Folly: Madness Lake.
The sign still reads 'Caution: year-round snow'
but the floes are thin water –

has it really been nine months?

'Madness Lake' – The name of Le Lac de Folly near Samoëns, France, suggests *Le lac de la folie*: the Lake of Madness.

Cristaux de Roche

Their gleam haunts my sleep:
the rocks and ores
from my grandmother's trove
in her loft at Lausanne.

When she heard that the clast
in her breast was cancer,
she willed them to me –
they lie dormant
in the box under my bed.

Relics of her grandfather Resteau,
the one with the alpenstock
and geologist's hammer.
My thoughts trail him

up Monts to the cusps
of Spitzen and Corni,
as I touch the points
of clustered quartz, a tiny massif.

Our forebear's dip-pen copperplate
names *sphène* and *galène*,
his labels mapping each to its origins.

We're family, but a man
of his Victorian inkhornisms
would be *vous* to me,
the accented stranger
who picks through his dusty specimens.

Nights, they take root in bedrock:
I see them grow to towering altitudes
of névé and depth-hoar.

Waking, I polish the facets
of a feldspar spire,
cup its lucent Matterhorn
in my palms.

Alexandre Resteau, Geologist *Manqué*

His treasures: eyeflash of tourmaline
        in a matrix of white,

glim of *gwindel* crystals
        their shade a warlock's smokescreen,

an iron rose, the weight
        of angular petals,

the blood-lustre garnet
        a dark vein between us.

I turn them between my fingers
and see a man with my eyes
make the slow climb from Göschenen to Airolo
across the divide between rivers,
the watershed of languages.

He sips a Ticino red at the Ospizio –
nerves steadier, he hauls on
boots and rubberised Mackintosh,
the miner's lamp still quavering in one hand.

The *cristallier* unfurls the rope ladder
and my grandmother's grandfather
shins down to the blind-end fissure –
squirms his head and shoulders
into the cavity of mineral fangs.

An hour later, he emerges,
whiskers thick with dust,
face beaming. In his hand,
a dusty lump of spikes.

He returns to Evian
with the worst torticollis
his doctor has ever seen
and *du quartz fumé magnifique.*

His peeling specimen-label reads
St Gotthard, 1859.
Still, his careful hand beckons
in sepia ink, to the keyhole pass.

Vésuve, 1857

The summits? *Qu'ils s'en aillent au diable!*
What lured him to the Alps at Pfeffers,
Monte Somma's rugged mezzaluna,
lay in their cores.

My ancestor Resteau
trudged in his sack-coat
up Vesuvius' cinder cone,
into the reeking crater.

He gathered igneous fallout
from the last explosion:
rusty pumice, light as a sponge.
A palm-sized lava bomb
the shape of a doll's crib.

Did he know they'd barely cooled
since the latest eruption?
Had he watched the guide
lower a choking dog
into the mountain's brimstone vapours?

I unwrap a snaggletoothed
jaw of yellow crystals.
A century and a half
since he collected them, and still
that hellmouth whiff of sulphur.

Galène

The jewel of his collection:
this sheet of slate with its galena cubes
glossily dense,

its weight a plumb-line
drawing it back underground.
Its motherlode at La Grave

is at two thousand metres –
we drag ourselves uphill in harness.
Our guide opens the creaking vault:

the drip of seeping water.
We walk into a darkness
that makes our eyes bulb blindly.

By torchlight, rusting hydraulics,
a minecart flaking with oxide.
The wall sweats damp and flowstone –

I think of corded sinews
hefting a pickaxe,
about the unknown miner

who found these crystals –
did he drink this oozing water
with its stale mineral smell?

How did he teeter down the slope
when the ice came?
Great-great grandfather,

it's not your smooth surveyor's palms
I think of, as the lead ore draws
the heat from my fingers.

I see hands chapped by frost,
calloused from the pick.

Above the Northeast Shoulder

Face the flawless white
of profound frostbite,
she stoops at the porch of my tent,
pale hair brushing my forehead.
One hand touches my arm,
scaldingly cold.

She points to the western arête –
a fin with skirls of cloud
building its north face
to a shell of rime.

That night, I arrange
my oxygen bottles, hunch
under canvas, and wait
for clear sky over the Lhotse Face.
She unzips the tent-flap
and lets in a swirl of blizzard.

She sits writing
a one-cigarette poem
by torchlight, brow knitting.

As the temperature drops
she creeps into my sleeping bag –
her kiss sucks the air from my lungs.
I spend all night trying to thaw her.

In the morning,
the pad propped on her knees,
she begins a two-fag poem.
I pass her my Zippo.

'*A two-fag poem*': Norman MacCaig joked self-deprecatingly
that his poems took him either one or two cigarettes to write.

Solo

for 'Jags'

Nieves penitentes,
those priestly pillars of snow,
nod their steepled heads as you pass:
a lone figure, stark on the Andean glacier.

A continent away, you taught me
the language of icefall and chimney,
hex, axe, cam, cwm –

now, your friend at Moraine Camp
lies sick with the rarefied air
of five thousand above.

But you have risen
an hour after midnight
to slog on, solo, your abandoned rope
a *quipu* tallying your twenty-two years,
uncoiling your final hours.

No snow-anchor to halt your fall,
no mastiff to yelp at crevasses,
paw at your icebound form.

Just lens-shaped cumulus
over neighbouring peaks,
and, from the east,
an approaching wall of storm.
Your breath, becoming cloud.

Encompassed

Between Arnos Grove and Gospel Oak
I'm haplessly lost, although
I can trace my own footprints
back through pathless forests.

This network of tunnels
sends my bearings spinning –
the crowd shunts me
through the airlessness of London Bridge,

but that sooty mouse still pinpoints
each crumb by the live rail,
skitters down the vertical wall
to its trackside bolthole.

Then, I remember Dad's compass
stowed in my holdall –
cardinal points clear, although
the rocks have scuffed its face.

I watch its needle tremble for north
and in the globe and orbit of its rose
I glimpse his wanderings
from Caracas to Muscat,

the powerful pull of the Home Counties.
I'm a hundred metres below pavements
but the city sprawls its grimy acres,
carved by the river, across my mind's map –

that sculpted dial by Tower Bridge
becoming a windrose,
and the electric glare
at the summit of the Shard
pointing north.

Translating Mountains from the Gaelic

A pebble on the tongue –
my clumsy mouth stumbles their meanings:

I mumble Beinn Laoghail to Ben Loyal,
Beinn Uais to Ben Wyvis,

humble Beinn Artair
from King Arthur's Hill to The Cobbler –

turn Bod an Deamhain
from Demon's Penis to Devil's Point,

stammer on An Teallach
with its rearing anvils and impossible spelling,

my throat a stream-gorge
where quartz chunks chatter against each other –

my English rolling off their sharp consonants.

Next summer, I'll shoulder my red rucksack,
a Platypus bottle, and a vial of Dad's ash

up Schiehallion –
Fairy-Hill of the Caledonians –
via the less-worn path.

A deerfly, its eyes peridot ringstones,
will pincer my skin for blood,

my voice a trespasser,
echoing charred moors and razed crofts.

Dad, I'll pour your English dust
for the hungry roots of the hill's oldest pine –

a speck of you will lodge in a walker's boot-tread,
the breeze catching a mote of your collarbone,

the rain will seep through you,
mingle you with Aonach Bàn,
Loch Teimheil, Sìdh Chailleann.

Ascent

All the dead come striding
from Steall Falls

and Coire Eòghainn,
up Jacob's Ladder

to Coire an t-Sneachda,
and the ice chandeliers

in Surgeon's Gully –
shoulder to shoulder

up the Hill of the Creel
and the Cliff of the Stag,

inching across
the Aonach Eagach

and Trotternish Ridge.
They shed wrenched crampons

and shivered bones,
rise from their falls,

ascending together
with spindrift hair

and mica eyes,
until they stand

on a single peak.
A snowlit land

rolls out before them
and the whiteout

lifts into light

Acknowledgements

Many thanks to the editors of the following magazines, in which some of these poems were previously published: *Mslexia, Shearsman, Stand, The Compass*. 'Alexandre Resteau, *Geologist Manqué*' was commended in the 2016 *Ambit* summer competition, 'Howlet' was highly commended in the 2016 Battered Moons competition, and 'Sexton Beetle, Glen Feshie' was highly commended in the 2016 York Literature Festival competition.

I am very grateful to poets and friends who have encouraged me with this project, especially Grevel Lindop, Helen Mort, Pascale Petit, Eleanor Rees and David Wilson.

I would like to acknowledge the support of a Northern Writer's Award from New Writing North, and a research grant from the University of Central Lancashire.

Special thanks go Vasilis Papageorgiou and Lo Snöfall for translating 'Alexandre Resteau, Geologist *Manqué*' and other mountain-poems into Greek and Swedish for *Chromata* magazine. I am indebted to Eilidh Scammell at Ainmean-Àite na h-Alba – Gaelic Place Names of Scotland – for helping me to research the meaning of place-names near the Grey Corries.